5 Steps To A Successful Re-Entry

❖❖❖❖❖❖❖❖❖❖❖❖❖❖❖❖

Clarence Bowden

ISBN 978-1-64258-350-2 (paperback)
ISBN 978-1-64299-181-9 (hardcover)
ISBN 978-1-64258-351-9 (digital)

Christian Faith Publishing, Inc.
832 Park Avenue
Meadville, PA 16335
www.christianfaithpublishing.com

All illustrations are courtesy of Pixbay

Printed in the United States of America

This book is dedicated to my
daughters *Nekia* and *Brittany*.

I would like to thank my wife Sandra (Bebe) for being my partner and the cement that held it all together during some very dark days and nights.

Acknowledgments

I would like to acknowledge and thank all the men and women making it possible for the much-needed help, and services delivered to those suffering from addictive disorders, mental illness and trauma; including all of you who have assisted *me.*

I would also like to acknowledge the individuals listed below who have assisted my becoming the Clinical Director I am today;

Richie Falzone
*Ed Greaux
*Eddie Hill
*Napoleon Johnson
Ulysses Kilgore
Dr. Monica Sweeney
*Derrick Whitter
Ronald Williams

*RIP

Author -
Clarence Bowden

✠✠✠✠✠✠✠✠✠✠✠✠✠

Coming home from a prison or jail sentence is a serious event that requires many things. An individual in this predicament has to have answers and basic needs met. There is a need for understanding, compassion, financial assistance, and emotional support. For the individuals who continue to recidivate much more is needed. Within the pages of this book are 5 steps that can assist with that process and make this trip home from incarceration the *last one.*

Introduction

I started writing my book the "5 Steps to a Successful Re-Entry" back in 2009. At the time I was working in HIV Services at a medium sized health center in Brooklyn NY. I had been there about 3 years when I began seeing former clients I had worked with in Outpatient Services years earlier. That program was for individuals on work release. This is a form of supervision for well-behaved incarcerated individuals granted a level of freedom to work in the community. As they began attending the center I noticed that most of their stories had the same outcome. They at first completed work release. This was followed by maxing out on parole. Followed by a return to prison with a new charge and steeper sentence. Some of them also now being infected with HIV disease. As I listened and provided care I began writing about what was being said to me. I also noticed that many of them had this resolve, which I identified as acceptance. It came across as if these clients had given in to returning to prison as being pre-determined and they could do nothing about it. Having gone down that path myself years earlier. I began to investigate what services were currently available for those returning to the community from prison. I also continued with my writing and had already accumulated a lot of material. Fast forward to August 2016. I am now working again in the drug treatment field as Clinical Director of a treatment center. I had not done anything with any of the writings outside of thinking that I wanted to put all of them into a book. One afternoon while recuperating in the hospital, after a six and half hour surgery to remove a tumor. My surgeon entered the room and informed me that I had Stage Three Colon Cancer. It took a few weeks for this to be digested. At my next appointment with him I was informed that I had the choices of chemotherapy or radiation either having to be done soon. It was during this time I began to do a lot of reflecting. I also started putting a lot of things in order. In September 2016 I started a somewhat new targeted chemotherapy treatment called Folfox. Being on chemo gave me the time and opportunity to put my writings in some order. In May 2017 I felt confident enough to have it copyrighted. My book was coming to life. As the "5 Steps to a Successful Re-Entry went to print this past February, I can say that I am currently cancer free and very hopeful for what my future holds. The book is a direct, easy to read, solution focused and very personal approach to addressing recidivism. Although written to help the incarcerated and formerly incarcerated, it is also for their families and the communities these men and women will be returning to. My hopes are that the "5 Steps to a Successful Re-Entry" achieves that goal.

Recidivism

Recidivism is the act of a person repeating an undesirable behavior after they have either experienced negative consequences of that behavior or have been trained to <u>extinguish</u> that behavior.

Step 1:

"Reality and Wake-up Call –
You Are Going Home"

This step is about the realization that you are finally going home. As you face this reality, think back to the last few weeks before your release. What was going through your mind? What promises did you make to yourself? Are you ready to keep them? How bad was your jail or prison stay? Did you really do the time standing on your head or did it go by with some problems? What was your reality of jail? You need to think about this when the times get difficult back in society and the feelings of giving up start showing up. Calm down, and begin the process of *unlearning* the thinking and behavior of getting over, giving up, blaming, not trusting, and being afraid of change. Learn to ask and seek appropriate *available* help, and do keep that first Parole / Probation appointment. I remember each and every time I went to jail, I felt fear that at any moment I would be involved in some sort of violence or abuse by the correction officers or other inmates like myself. I remember once while in Great Meadows (Comstock) back in 1977 seeing a man get a blanket pulled over him and being hit in the head with various objects.

I could see that some of the objects were socks with who knows what inside of them. (As you know these things happen quickly and the violence can be fatal. They can be for something minor, or some other perceived disrespect / or other cause). This resulted in the individual being laid completely out and my seeing blood seeping from underneath the blanket. All the while with not one guard in sight. Another time I got sucker punched and had to fight off two individuals thinking that I was an easy target. It is during these times a shank came in handy if you get my meaning. Throughout the years on so many occasions witnessing and experiencing so much violence, you would have thought I would have said no more. *Not a chance*! I was released on Oct 24, 1978 from Arthur Kill Correctional Facility at age twenty after being transferred from Great Meadows. I immediately resumed the criminal activity of selling drugs and larceny I was involved with prior to incarceration. To return home from a multi-year prison bid to only repeat the cycle that got you there is lunacy. Most of you reading this have already experienced this. It is time to wake up and to stay woke.

Step 2:

"Getting Needs Met"

Hold it! Watch out for the welcome home celebrations and the well meaning family members and friends. This includes the toxic ones as well. You know who they are. They are the ones who will offer you that first shot of dope, a drink, a snort of coke, pull of the stem, or drag of the joint. They are also the ones that will offer you the chance of a lifetime (again) to get that "money". Believe me you will definitely be interested. I was! In fact I acted on it immediately. One of the times I came home from Rikers Island in the early 80's. My so-called homies had a little party for me. Afterward we went out and robbed an innocent victim. For me it meant nothing at all. When I look back now, I was like that caterpillar following the leader into the fire. You have to follow your plan when released and if you don't have one, get one and fast. Many individuals coming home from an incarceration fail the *very first day* due to this not being in place. Having a plan will make things so much easier and will keep you from many of the pitfalls waiting for you.

It is a best practice to have this plan in place <u>before</u> your release. The following needs must be addressed. There is no excuse for your not being able to incorporate most of these items into your re-entry plan. Failing to do so will sabotage your re-entry and it will only be a matter of time before you are returned to jail with a new charge or a violation. Must haves and *keys* for your successful return are as follows:

- housing (family, friends, SRO, half - way houses)
- supportive services (parole/probation and any of the mandates returnees are required to see once released)
- employment, public assistance and/or family support (if available)
- mental health services, drug treatment (residential or outpatient) whichever is needed
- vocational and educational services
- medical follow up care including HIV testing
- resource guides and phone numbers to the free hotlines offering assistance
- know what your triggers are
- have patience
- take your medication(s) as prescribed and refill appropriately
- do not panic because of drug using dreams (When they come speak with someone, they are a part of the recovery process)
- sexual intercourse is okay, just relax about it and use protection
- let your past go and live the new you
- it's okay to cry

Step 3:

"Reality"

Goodbye *delusional thinking*. This means taking those ideas to come out for that one big score or package and throwing them in the garbage where they belong. There are no big packages or scores left for you. Until you understand this you are already defeated and on your way back for another bid. What will it be this time, one year, four to twelve, six to eighteen, life?

After all of the time spent incarcerated and seeing so many individuals return to prison or being killed; your goal is still to go back to the neighborhood and do it again. So here is how that works. You are released to the community and you either go to a family member, or that girlfriend met as a pen pal whom you were introduced too by one of your cellmates. For the first few days and even weeks you are joyful and basking in the freedom you have gained. Soon anxiety sets in as the funds you had begin to run out. This realization causes serious stress and places you in a negative frame of mind. You are faced with this dilemma. Should I ignore my parole stipulations and go back to the block where the action is? Should I find a job? You think to your-self, how much money will I make? What kind of work can I do? Where will I find it? I will say this, going back to the block and the old neighborhood to resume the street life of selling drugs or the sticking up of innocent people is not the way.

You can believe this; if you did not obtain that pot of gold when you were out on the streets before incarceration, then that time has now passed you by. It is time to wake up and do something different. Why not? Times are hard for many people. They are even harder for an individual with a criminal record. It is not the end of the world. You do not have to behave like it is. Step back and give yourself a **time out.** Take this time to think before taking any action. Recognize the pain and the discomfort that will surely be present. These feelings will eventually fade and allow you to make a better decision. Do not be afraid (or ashamed)

to seek help every step of the way. It is a delusion to think that you are going to turn back time, and make that "real money" you always thought would come your way.

The real money will come from hard work. Step 4 speaks to putting those successful things done in the past to work for you now. This means not selling drugs, sticking up innocent people or any other criminal activity that will send you back to jail. It does means being motivated, dedicated, and hardworking with a sense of survival that is positive. I often ask individuals I am treating if they remember their very 1st arrest. Most of them say they do. Others say that it was too long ago. I also ask what was it like being arrested again and going back to the jail they had previously left. For me I remember being welcomed as if I had went on some journey and was returning like some hero. I received cartons of Newport cigarettes, hugs and pats on the back. I was told by others of there being so much laughter and talk of old times. The discussion of the new charges also becomes of interest and the "jailhouse lawyers" have their say about what you should do. You begin to listen to them and soon start thinking of taking a plea deal to get it over. You are afraid of going to trial. You know that this being you're second or third felony, what is in store if you lose the trial. As mentioned earlier what sentence will it be this time? Meanwhile back in the community your family now has to survive (again) without you. What are they to do? Should they begin stealing, selling drugs, committing robberies, or become prostitutes to get money for you to get out if a bail is offered? Do they go to the block where your homies are and ask for help? Is there a cost for this help? Wait a minute! These are your homies and everything is supposed to be cool; right? Your significant other, wife, husband or child can just go and pick up whatever is needed without any strings attached, hmmmm? What happens when the assistance does not come? What do you do then? These scenarios take place over and over and over again.

Yet you are still willing to place yourself and family in its path once more. The term insanity as it relates to the recovery community is expecting a different result for the very same behavior. This is what yours (and mine) looked like at one time. It is up to you to end the insanity. Just as I have.

Step 4:

"Working It"

How much success did you have doing your "thing"? Did you forget the skills that helped you survive the streets for so long? This step is about looking over these skills and taking the **best of them** for your new and positive lifestyle change. The same drive you had to stay up for days on end searching for a victim. The dedication that you put on that corner for the dollar at all times of the day and night. This was true survival; forget that you had a need for a drug or a place to stay. I see so many individuals from my past on the streets or when I visit shelters and programs. Some of them suffer from serious mental health disorders. Others have medical conditions that prevent them from doing much. I also frequently see the other side. These are the guys I see driving by who wave at me from their cars as they go about their business. They decided that another way was best and took it. Work, family and all of the positive things they decided to do instead of that unfruitful and dangerous old game which has been played out for so long. Just take a look at who are running that game we played now. They are young, bold, crafty non-caring individuals who are mostly gang-bangers or gangsters. They are smart and very ruthless. I am not saying old timers like you and I were soft. I am saying our time has passed and we have children their ages, some of whom may even be a part of their gangs. When does the role modeling that we are supposed to have been doing take place? How does it feel looking into the eyes of your children or grandkids? What about your wife or significant other? Nothing is lost on them. They know the deal! What will it do to them if you were to catch another bid? I repeat take the best out of what was used to survive so long on the streets and put it to use in a *positive and meaningful* way. You are not promised anything other than a chance that is up to you to take and make the best of. Roll with the frustrations like you rolled with the bad days and most importantly do not give up on yourself again.

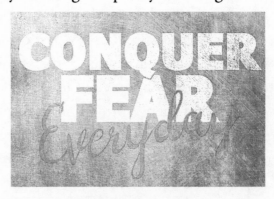

Remember those times when you said to yourself "I am not leaving this corner or going home without getting some money". This has to translate now into "I will go into every store, interview for any job and do whatever it takes to put food on the table for me and my family without committing anymore crimes. I am staying out of jail for good and this time *I will succeed*!

Step 5:

"Getting It Done"

This last step is about believing in *yourself* to get it right this time around. Practice how to get through a bad day and the feelings that it creates. What can you do on days like these? Where can you go? Again, it is not the end of the world. Develop a *personal* mission statement that will get you through the hard times and those negative feelings of poor me, I can't do it, I'm trying and nothing is happening. These are self defeating statements that must be turned around. "I can, I will, I have" is the new motto to live by now. You are in the driver's seat to finally place a real *value* on your freedom and life. I had to internalize what I really wanted. I also had help from a smart woman who had her head on right. I was not ready for the relationship and eventually sabotaged it. I did learn a great deal about myself from her. Out of the relationship my first child was born. This was one of the milestones in my life. However it did not stop my criminal thinking, behavior and drug use. After the relationship ended I was fortunate to meet someone else and she became my first wife. From that relationship my second child was born. Again this did not totally stop my addiction and criminal behavior. It took a combination of all of the loss and internal pain that forced me to take a real look at myself to see that I had enough. In January 1989 despite all of that, I was arrested again. This was to be the *last* time.

The arrest introduced me to drug treatment as an alternative to incarceration. I accepted and surrendered to it. It saved my life and gave me a career and a way to pay back some of the damage I did to my family and community. It also put me in contact with some very smart people who mentored and showed me that there was another way. I also learned about some of the root causes of my repeated behavior and reasons for it. This was learning that I had been traumatized from early on. From my childhood up until a good part of my adult life I had been either a victim or a witness to events that were traumatizing. I had to learn what being traumatized meant. This opened my eyes to so many areas within myself and allowed me to grow emotionally. You have to learn how this important effect on your brain had on your development, and made you the person you are today. Being Trauma Informed helps you understand that there is a link between your substance use and the trauma you have experienced in your life. You also must understand that in order for the substance abuse to end the trauma experienced by you must be treated. Often times this needs to be done simultaneously. I have an equation that I often share with people and it goes like this Honesty + Commitment = Change. It challenges you to dig deep and take responsibility for the actions of your behavior and change it.

Each of us make our own paths; however we all need a road map or guide to follow. Following these basic 5 steps can be that guide and assist your chances for success a great deal. Remember to be humble, to have hope and most importantly believe and trust that a *successful re-entry* is yours for the taking. *Relaxing + Thinking = Positive Decision Making.* This guide was developed to assist with that process. That old saying "The life you save may be your own" comes to mind here. Freedom from incarceration is a beautiful thing and the only way it will happen for you is to do the work it requires.

I have since remarried and have a wife I can call a partner. This year (2018) will make 20 years of marriage for us. It has been a journey well worth taking. I cannot promise that you will receive the same things I have. However I can assure you that they can be, if you work hard, and take what has been offered you within the pages of this book.

Epilogue

You have just finished reading the *5 Steps* and there is still some convincing needed on the necessity for you to change. Follow me on this;

This is what you have – friends, family and maybe some money.

This is what Law Enforcement has – multiple data banks, vehicles, weapons, finances, manpower, informants, and support from the community. This is the reality you are up against. When do you accept that going against societal norms and your criminal behavior and thinking has to end? Get out of your own way and stop living with a closed fist. You have to open that fist. What have you got to lose?

You can do this.

Resource Guide

311 NYC Services

NYC Commission on Human Rights (CCHR)
40 Rector Street (10th Flr).
New York, NY 10006
212-306-7450

NYC Department of Citywide Administrative Services (DCAS)
1 Centre St. 17th Floor South
New York, NY 10007
212- 669-7000

NYC Department of Correction (DOC)
For general inquiries, call the DOC
Information Line at: 718-546-1500 (open 24/7)
For an inmate medical emergency, call Prison
Health Services: 718-546-5200 (open 24/7)

NYC Department of Health and Mental Hygiene (DOHMH)
125 Worth St.
New York, NY 10013
Call 311 for nearest center.
Services: Transitional Health Care
Coordination (THCC)

NYC Department of Homeless Services (DHS)
33 Beaver St.
New York, NY 10004
Client Advocacy: 1-800-994-6494
General: 212-361-8000

NYC Department of Probation (DOP)
33 Beaver St.
New York, NY 10004

NYC Housing Authority (NYCHA)
Application offices:
55 West 125th St., 7th Fl.
Manhattan/Queens
1 Fordham Plaza, 5th Fl.

NYC Human Resources Administration (HRA) / Department of Social Services
180 Water St.
New York, NY 10038
HRA Info Line at: 1-877-472-8411

Legal and other Resources

ACCES – VR
1 -800 -222 – JOBS (5627)

Alpha School / Center for Progressive Living, Inc.
2400 Linden Blvd.
Brooklyn, NY 11208
(718) 257-5800

Bronx Defenders
860 Courtland Ave.
Bronx, NY 10451
(800) 597-7980
(718) 838-7878

Brooklyn Chamber of Commerce
335 Adams St #2700, Brooklyn, NY 11201
(718) 875-1000

CAMBA
2211 Church Ave., Rm 307
Brooklyn, NY 11226
(718) 282-0108

Center for Employment Opportunities (CEO)
32 Broadway, 15th Fl.
New York, NY 10004
(212) 422-4430

Counseling Services of the Eastern District of New York (CSEDNY)
180 Livingston St., Suite 301
Brooklyn, NY 11201
(718) 858-6631 ext. 10

Doe Fund / Ready Willing & Able
520 Gates Ave.
Brooklyn, NY 11216
(646) 672-4273

The Door - A Center of Alternatives
555 Broome St.
New York, NY 10013
(212) 941-9090

DYC (Dynamite for Youth)
1830 Coney Island Ave
Brooklyn NY 11230
(718) 376- 7923

El Regreso, Inc. (Spanish Language Treatment)
728 Driggs Ave.
Brooklyn, NY 11211
(718) 384-6400

Federation Employment and Guidance Services (F.E.G.S)
199 Jay St.
Brooklyn, NY 11201
(718) 488-0100 ext. 436
Infoline: (212) 524-1780

Fortune Society
26-76 Northern Blvd.
Long Island City, NY 11101
(212) 691-7554

Goodwill Industries of Greater NY and Northern NJ, Inc.
Centers in Queens, Bronx, and Brooklyn
(718) 728-5400

Greenhope Services for Women, Inc.
448 East 119th St.
New York, NY 10035
(212) 369-5100

Hope Center Nursing (HIV Services Provider)
1401 University Ave Bronx NY 10452
(718) 408 -6333

Incarcerated Mothers Program
Edwin Gould Services for
Children
1968 2nd Ave.
New York, NY 10029
(646) 315-7600

Kings County Hospital Center
451 Clarkson Ave.
Brooklyn, NY 11203
(718) 245-2660

Kings County Re-Entry TASC Force
210 Joralemon Street Bklyn NY 11201
(718) 250 -3281
Reentry@brooklynda.org

Legal Information for Families (LIFT)
350 Broadway, Suite 501
New York, NY 10013
(646) 613-9633

Legal Action Center
225 Varick St., 4th Fl.
New York, NY 10014
(212) 243-1313
(800) 223-4044 Toll Free

Legal Aid Society
Main Number
(212) 577-3300
Criminal Division
111 Livingston St.
Brooklyn, NY 11210
(718) 237-2000

MCM Faith, Inc.
658 Jamaica Ave.
Brooklyn, NY 11208
(866) 552-0500 Toll Free

Neighborhood Defender Services of Harlem
317 Lenox Ave., 10th Fl.
New York, NY 10027
(212) 876-5500

New Directions of Brooklyn NY
202-206 Flatbush Ave.
Brooklyn, NY 11217
(718) 398-0800

Nontraditional Employment for Women (N.E.W.)
243 West 20th St.
New York, NY 10011
(212) 627-6252

OASAS
(518) 457 -7077
oasas.gov

Odyssey House
219 East 121st St.
New York, NY 10035
(212) 987-5100

Office of Vocational and Educational Services for Individuals with Disabilities

NYS Education Department (VESID)
55 Hanson Place, 2nd Fl.
Brooklyn, NY 11217
(800) 222-5627
www.vesid.nysed.gov

Osborne Association
(718) 707-2600
(800) 344-3314 (Family Helpline)

Palladia, Inc.
Admissions
(718) 294-4184
(212) 979-8800

Phoenix House of New York

(212) 831-1555

(800) 4357-111 ext. 7500

Samaritan Village

88-83 Van Wyck Expressway

Jamaica, NY 11435

(718) 657-8010

(800) 532-HELP Toll Free

Stay 'N Out Programs – NY Therapeutic Communities. Inc

1 - Serendipity I (Men)

2071 Fulton Street

Brooklyn, NY 11233

(718) 398-0096

Fax: (347) 770-8654

2 - Serendipity II (Women)

944 Bedford Avenue

Brooklyn, NY 11205

(718) 802-0572

Fax: (718) 802-9885

3 - NYTC Brooklyn Outpatient Program
2071 Fulton Street
Brooklyn NY 11233
(718) 398 -0096
Fax: (347) 770 -8649

4 - NYTC Queens Outpatient Program
162 -24 Jamaica Ave (Lower Level)
Jamaica NY 11432
(718) 657 -2021
Fax: (718) 657 -0299

Re-Entry Bureau
210 Joralemon Street
Brooklyn NY 11201
(718) 250 -3281

Supportive Training Results In Valuable Employees (STRIVE)

East Harlem Employment Services, Inc.
240 East 123 St., 3rd Fl.
New York. NY 10035
(212) 360-1100
(646) 335-0814

Wildcat Service Corporation
2 Washington Street, 3rd Flr
New York, NY 10004
(212) 209-6000

Women In Need, Inc. (WIN)
Intake
455 Decatur St.
Brooklyn, NY 11233
(718) 453-2190 ext. 116

Women's Prison Association
110 Second Ave.
New York, NY 10003
(646) 292-7740

Workforce1
625 Fulton St.
Brooklyn, NY 11201
(718) 780-9200

National Resources

National Addiction Hotline
1(888) 352 -6072

SAMHSA
National Drug Treatment locator
1 (800) 662 -4357

Housing

Volunteers of America
1660 Duke Street
Alexandria VA 22314
(703) 341 -5000

Mental Health Services

(SAMHSA) Treatment Referral Helpline at 1-800-662-HELP (4357)
1(800) life – Net (543 -3638)

National Resources

Drug Treatment Services
OASAS
(518) 457 -7077
oasas.gov

*All resources can be found online. There is also a free booklet called – "Turning the Game Around" by The NYC Commission on Human Rights. Copies are free to the formerly incarcerated. Contact NYC Commission on Human Rights, 40 Rector Street, New York NY 10006 or call 311 for a copy.

Although many of the resources listed are for New York State. You can also receive information for your state by contacting The Chamber of Commerce in *your* state or any of the National Hotlines. ***Resources are available.***

Biography

Clarence Bowden is a Credentialed Alcohol Substance Abuse Counselor (**CASAC**) and a Certified Recovery Peer Advocate (**CRPA**), with 30 plus years of combined personal and professional experience in criminal justice. He is presently the Clinical Director of Serendipity 1, which is one of the premier programs in the NYC area. Mr. Bowden is also a trainer for CASAC – T students studying to become credentialed counselors and is the past Deputy Director of Work Release for the Phoenix House Outpatient Center and a former New York City Dept of Health AIDS Hotline Counselor during the height of the epidemic. Mr. Bowden will be married 20 years this coming November 2018 and the father of 2 adult daughters who are also professionals in their respective fields.

Contact information – twitter - @bluesky51, email - cbchooselife@yahoo.com

CPSIA information can be obtained
at www.ICGtesting.com
Printed in the USA
FFOW02n1649060718
47275526-50195FF